# INSPIRATIONAL QUOTATIONS

by Samuel M. Dickerson

ISBN: 9798330220076

Printed in the United States of America

# ACKNOWLEDGEMENTS

First and foremost, I'd like to say thanks to everyone that helped inspire me to write this book. I'd like to thank all the people that offered feedback and critiqued my work while I was still in the process of making my inspirational quotations book.

I'd like to thank my mother and my brother even though they're in Heaven watching over me.

Ma, love you and I want you to know that I'm still going to make you proud someday. I never got to buy you that big house I always wanted to, but I'm going to make you happy in other ways. I'm going to tell the world how special you are to me, and I'm going to tell them how much you loved God and Jesus.

To my brother, Skilly, love you, man. I wish you were here to read my book yourself and tell me what you think of it, but one day, we'll have that conversation. It might be on earth one day if God decides to bring you back. If not, it'll be in Heaven. One way or another, I know we'll see each other again. I miss you, bro, and I know you and Mommy are together in Heaven making everyone laugh. They say laughter is good for the soul,

AND ALL YOU EVER DID WAS MAKE PEOPLE LAUGH AND SMILE. YOU WAS A REAL JOKESTER. I MISS YOU SO MUCH.

THIS IS A MESSAGE TO MY CHILDREN. KEEP GOING FORWARD. DON'T NEVER LET NOBODY TELL YOU WHAT Y'ALL CAN'T DO. REACH FOR THE STARS, AND EVEN IF Y'ALL DON'T MAKE IT TO THE TOP RIGHT AWAY, KEEP REACHING FOR THE STARS. IT TOOK ME ALMOST 46 YEARS TO WRITE MY FIRST BOOK. IT WON'T TAKE Y'ALL THAT LONG IF Y'ALL STAY FOCUSED AND CHASE Y'ALL'S DREAMS. NOTHING IS IMPOSSIBLE WITH GOD BY YA'LL'S SIDE, Y'ALL CAN DO ANYTHING.

TO MY DAUGHTER BORN ON 5/28/1996, CHASE YOUR DREAM, BABY GIRL. DADDY LOVES YOU. I KNOW I MISSED A LOT OF YEARS OF YOUR LIFE, BUT DON'T THINK I LOVE YOU ANY LESS.

TO MY SON BORN ON 2/16/2009. I LOVE YOU. YOU'RE MY JUNIOR, BUT YOU DON'T HAVE TO FOLLOW IN MY FOOTSTEPS OR MAKE THE MISTAKES I MADE. YOU CAN BE SO MUCH MORE THAN I EVER WAS. THAT'S WHY I'M ALWAYS PUSHING YOU AND TELLING YOU TO TRY NEW THINGS AND STAY POSITIVE. I LOVE YOU.

TO MY OTHER SON BORN ON 9/8/2010, I LOVE YOU. YOU WANT TO KNOW SOMETHING? EVEN THOUGH I HAVEN'T BEEN THE BEST FATHER TO YOU BECAUSE I HAVEN'T BEEN THERE, I STILL WANT TO SEE YOU DO GREAT IN LIFE. YOU REALLY IMPRESS ME WITH THE CHOICES YOU MAKE. NOBODY'S

PERFECT. NOT ME, YOU, OR ANYBODY ELSE, BUT JUST CONTINUE TO STRIVE AND EVENTUALLY YOU'LL FIND WHAT YOUR PURPOSE IN LIFE IS. PRAY TO GOD AND ASK GOD TO SEND YOU SIGNS.

TO MY DAUGHTER BORN ON 10/20/2010, I LOVE YOU, SWEETHEART. YOU'RE MY BABY GIRL AND LIKE YOUR BROTHERS AND SISTER, I LOVE YOU TOO. ONE DAY, I'M GOING TO BE A PART OF YOUR LIFE. WE'LL BE ON BETTER TERMS. I LOVE YOU SO MUCH, AND I'M VERY PROUD OF YOU. YOUR MOTHER DID A GREAT JOB RAISING YOU. I USED TO LOVE TO DANCE WHEN I WAS YOUNG TOO. I WISH YOU COULD'VE SEEN HOW MANY MOVES I HAD. I LOVE YOU BABY GIRL. YOU'RE SO SMART. I'M ALWAYS PRAYING FOR YOU AND YOUR MOM. KEEP DOING GOOD. I'M GOING TO REWARD YOU ONE DAY, GOD WILLING!

BESIDES THAT, I'D LIKE TO THANK ALL MY MENTORS, BOTH POSITIVE AND NEGATIVE BECAUSE I LEARNT SO MUCH FROM JUST BEING OBSERVANT.

I'D LIKE TO SAY A SPECIAL THANKS TO ALL THE OTHER PEOPLE THAT HELPED MAKE THIS BOOK POSSIBLE.

I'D ALSO LIKE TO THANK DR. A. HELLER. YOU BELIEVED IN ME WHEN I DIDN'T EVEN BELIEVE IN MYSELF. THANK YOU. YOU'RE SOMEONE I'LL NEVER FORGET.

I'd like to thank A. Santoro. Thank you for treating me like a friend and always offering me advice. As you can see, I took it. You're also someone I'll never forget. Thank you very much. I hope you're still doing your thing.

I'd like to thank my God brother, S. Mosley. Thanks, bro. I really appreciate you. You're one of the realest dudes I've ever known, and I'm not just saying that. Thanks for all the feedback you've given me on my work.

To my first love. Thank you for teaching me what true love really is. I love you so much. I think about you every day, and I miss you so much. I wish you'd come back into my life so we could mend each other's broken hearts. I know you love me still. I can feel it in my bones. The love we share is special to me.

To all my past lovers. If I have any children I don't know about, just tell them I love them and encourage them to chase their dreams.

To my children's mothers, I love you, NM. I love you MY. I love you, TM. I'm so sorry.

To my sister, love you. I know we don't always see things eye to eye, but we're all we got left.

To my other 2 special sisters, SM and LC. Thank you for being there for me when I needed you the most.

To my cousin, UH, thank you, bro. I appreciate you. You've been there for me, and you're states away. I'll never forget that.

To my granddaughter, SM. I love you, little one.

To my little brothers, EC, TJ, TB, SL, thank you for believing in me and telling me to go forward. Thanks.

To all my other family members that told me I could make it, I appreciate the encouragement.

I would like to thank my best friend, NM. Thank you for everything you've done for me and for always being supportive regardless of what I've been going through.

Thank you to my cousin, DB. I really appreciate you, cousin. Thanks for being there for me.

# Introduction

I wouldn't have been able to write this book if it wasn't for all the knowledge I accumulated throughout the years. I didn't want to get too deep in my inspirational quotations' definitions, but I figured I'd let my readers hear a few of my inner thoughts. I hope you enjoy this book I made, and I hope that it opens your eyes to my view on life and different areas of life. I plan to one day turn these inspirational quotations into T-shirts as well. I want to make an honest living, and these are just two ways I plan to change my lifestyle.

Samuel M. Dickerson

Don't focus on what you can't do put barriers on your mind. Think outside the box. That's what thinking big is all about.

*Don't let outside forces, circumstances, or people stop you from loving who you love.*

Not everyone is loyal, so when you find someone that's loyal to you, be loyal to them.

Honor your mother and father and days shall be many. Honor your elders as well, but most of all, honor God.

You never know who you're entertaining or who's help you may need later on in life, so treat people equally.

There's no mountain love can't climb,
and no ocean love can't cross.

Some things are freely given, and some things you have to work for.

When I see something I want, I strive to get it because I'm a go getter. Don't let nothing or anyone stand in your way.

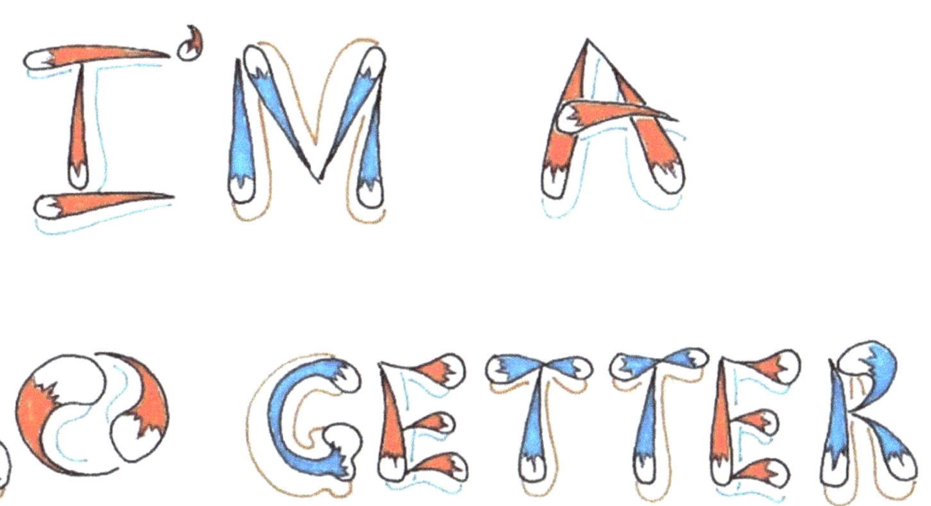

Be different.
Make everlasting impressions.
Don't follow the crowd.
Lead by example.

Learn to take risks.

Be courageous.

That's the only way you'll advance in life.

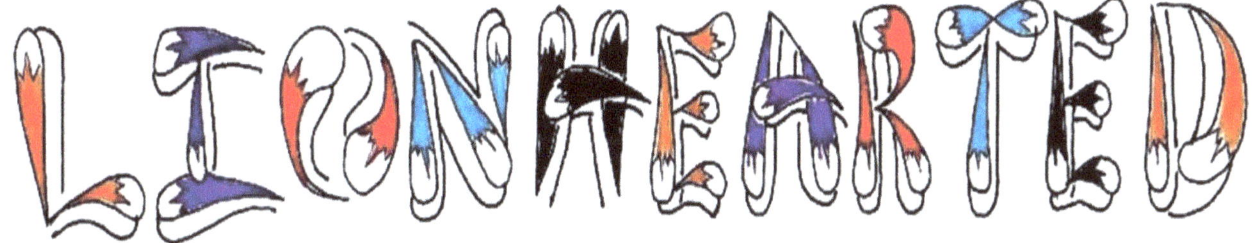

*If you fall, get up and go even harder.*

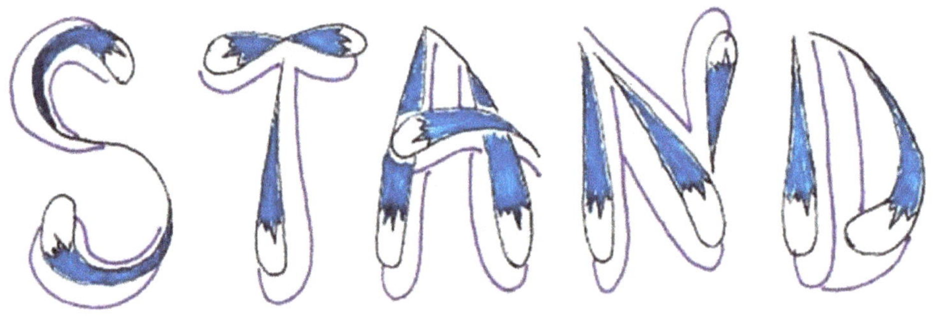


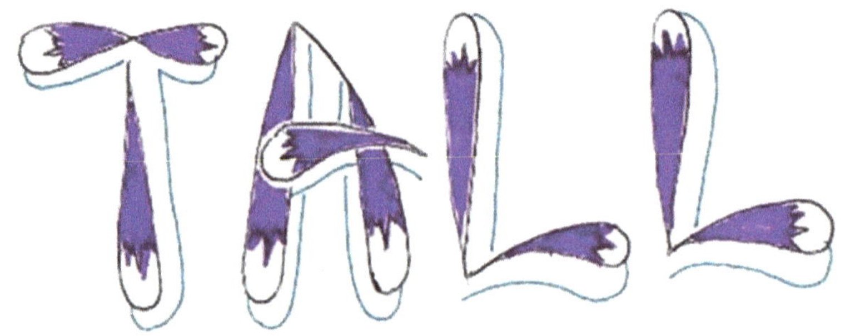

*Everybody misses someone, whether it's a mother, father, sister, brother, grandparent, aunt, uncle, or friend.*

You never know what to expect when you travel down the path called.

Even when the odds are against you,

Jesus said, "Don't worry about nothing."

It's a blessing just to know you've been

Don't sit around and wait for tomorrow to come to get your life together.

*Are you willing to travel that extra mile for what you believe in?*

It's time we sit down at the table, put our heads together, and come up with a plan that'll make all of our lives better.

Can you see the flames of love flickering in my eyes or feel the warmth of my heart?

I'M
IN
LOVE

Everything is subject to change and every relationship has its ups and down, so fight for what you love and love with all your heart.

This is my way of never saying goodbye.

Ask for help if you need help. Try not to wait until it's too late to reach out to your support network while you have the opportunity to do so.

Take care of your hygiene, wash your face, brush your teeth, change your clothes, be responsible, go to work, take care of your children, honor your mother and father, respect your significant other.

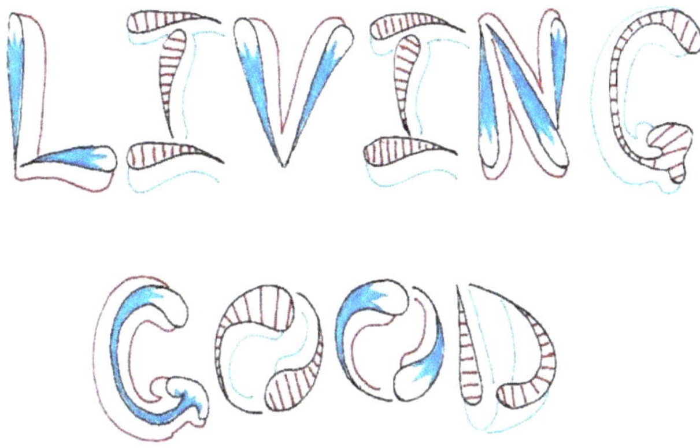
LIVING
GOOD

Show compassion, treat people how you want to be treated, and pray for others.

Think about all the things you have compared to the things you don't. Learn to be grateful for everything you've been given because every day

we live is a gift.

Be brave and face each day with optimistic eyes.

Never let nothing hold you back and if you have dreams, pursue them.

Everything takes time. Nothing happens overnight. If you keep on seeking, eventually you 'll see the light.

It's time we stop hurting, abusing, and killing each other. It's time we start loving, respecting, and lifting one another.

Let's learn to live and live and learn.
If we use our hearts and minds, the
world won't be the way that it is.

*Be grateful for every blessing you receive.*

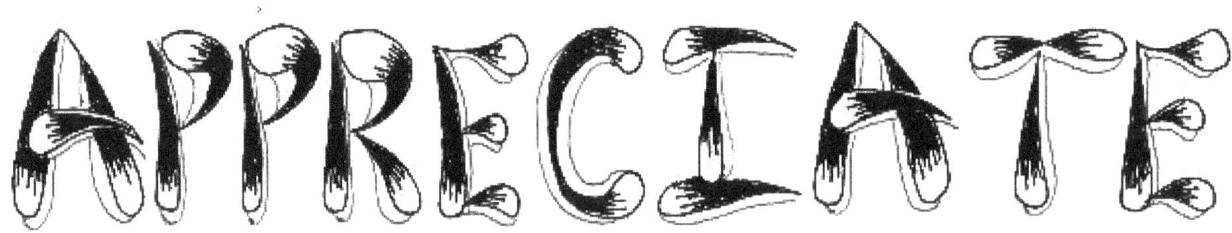

Heavenly Father, I ask that you would let your

You have to be willing to take risks to get where you want to be because life will test you. But when it all boils down, it's about

It took time for me to open up my heart, but eventually

Stand up to oppression.

We are all secretly seeking your face
and praying for your guidance.

I've been a dog lover all my life, and I always will be. Dogs are the best.

I'm in love with my feline friend.
My cat is so smart ~

When you find it, cherish it and don't let it go because

*I looked the Devil in the eyes and said,*

I'm hungry, and the only thing I want to catch is a

I'm not Christian, Protestant, or Catholic. I just believe in Christ. Many will be called. Only a few will be chosen.

There are no shortcuts to take around the paths of life. The only way to make it past your barriers is if you're willing to

# Happy Valentine's Day

It doesn't pay to stimulate your senses or impair your vision, but it pays to listen because all drugs and alcohol do is cause collisions.

Everybody craves one thing or another but deep down inside, I think we're all just

*Shout out to all the ballers that came out of Harlem*

The only thing holding a grudge is going to do is make you bitter.
Some people are addicted to sex, money, drugs, women...

What's your addiction?
Once you know what it is, that's the
first step to overcoming it!

Make the most of every day you're given.

Nonchalantly, I was watching you watch me.
I didn't say anything, but

Eventually, I have to find Heaven
because half my life, I feel like

When you feel like the pain is too much to bear, you're all alone, and you feel like giving up

Although I've made mistakes in the past, I continually remind myself every day that

When you find someone who makes
you feel like your life is worth living,
don't be afraid to say,

I'm ready for whatever tomorrow may bring and in time, I'll show the world I'm

S.I., rep your borough, shout out to Wu-Tang Clan, home of the 36 chambers.

*Regardless of what I'm going through, my trust is in the Lord.*

No matter how many times life knocks you down, get back up and keep on fighting.

It's not about how you start.
It's about how you finish.
If you want to be a success story, put
your heart, soul, and mind into
everything you do and see where it
leads you!!!

KEEP
THE
FAITH

Guide people when they need guidance.
Pray for others that need a prayer.
Teach people how to be better people.

It's easy to get sidetracked by the obstacles you face in life, but if you're determined to reach your destination,

Sometimes people are going to make you laugh. Other times people are going to make you cry.

Don't let negative thoughts contaminate your mind. Focus on what thoughts actually matter.

You can't serve God and serve Man at the same time. You have to make up your mind and decide who you're going to live for.

After all the blood, sweat, tears, trials, and tribulations, I'm surprised I'm

B.K., shake the building! Is Brooklyn
in the house?

I never worked for Uncle Sam. My life's been hell.

Ain't no shame in my game, yet proudly, I say, I was

It was the toughest fight I ever had to endure, but with God's help my faith in God, I can say,

B.X. Boogie Down Bronx Forever!
Represent your borough.

There ain't too many roads I haven't traveled. I got some stories to tell.

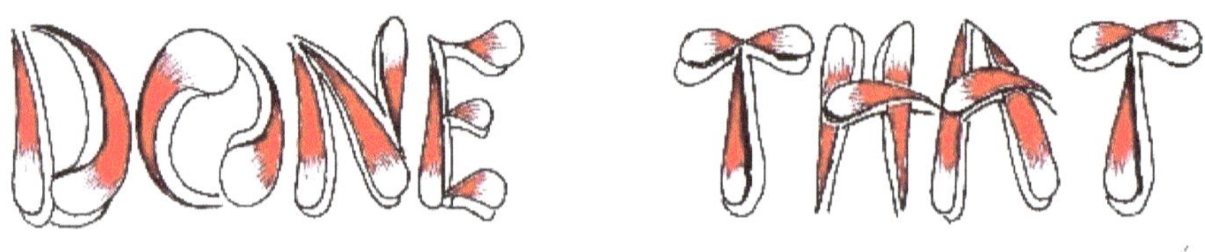

*If only you could see the things I saw and walk in my shoes for a few years, then you'd say,*

I'm not perfect, and in the past, I've sinned many times, but all I can say is,

Before I made it to the top, I envisioned it, so you could call me a

*L.I. (Strong Island), where y'all at?*
*Shout out to all my peoples!*

Studies have shown and proved that individuals not only think more accurately but also drive better when they're not under the influence of drugs or alcohol.

When something needs to get done and others won't rise to the occasion,

God gave each of us a heart so we could

Before others recognize the greatness in u, u have to recognize the greatness in yourself.
Think like a champion.

The only thing I'm trying to do is go forward in life. If you ain't trying to do likewise,

# A portrait taken of my love for you.

# Isn't this the perfect way to get your day started?

Start your day off with a smile towards others and a

Q.B., represent ya stomping grounds!!

"From the cradle to the grave."

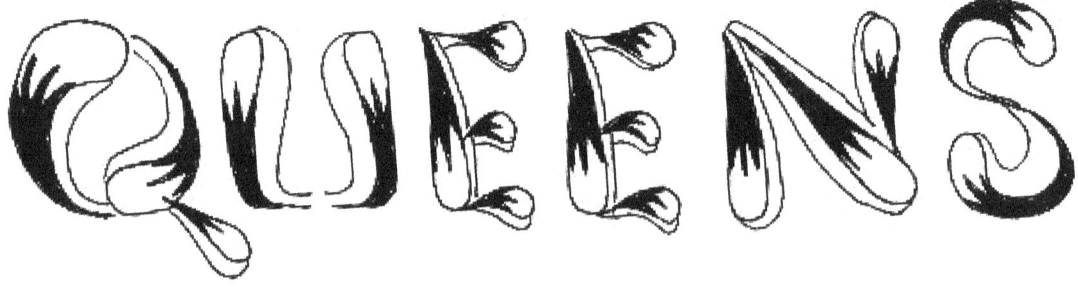

Don't be afraid to fly and remember
WE ALL GOT
WINGS

God is always with you in good times and in bad times, so try to remember you're never

God hears and answers the prayers of the

Every day, all day, I'm
BOSSED UP

If I wasn't in a relationship, I probably would give you my number, but unfortunately, I can't because

If you know you a baddie, don't be afraid to say, I'm a

 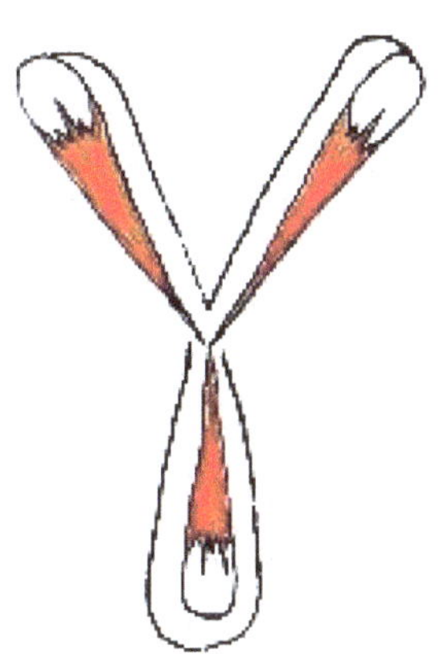 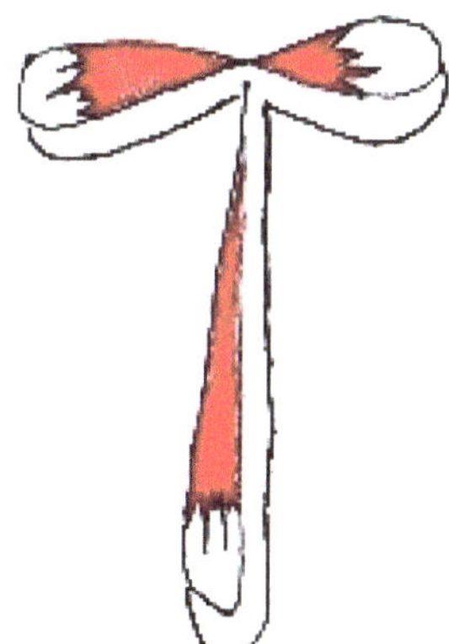

When you find yourself almost
reaching your breaking point,

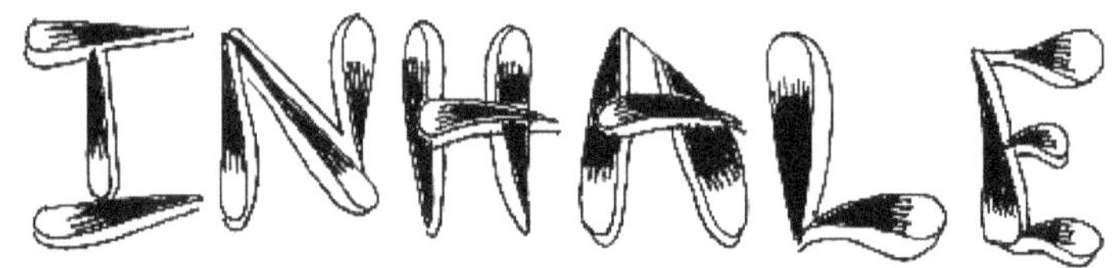

The blood of my ancestors runs through my veins.

My mother's my
NUMBER
ONE

It's OK to want to have nice things,
but always remember,

I'm not only a foreigner, I'm also a

Adam wasn't perfect. Eve wasn't perfect. And

Nowadays, everybody's trying to survive however they can. This is what I call

God, without you in my life, my life has no meaning.

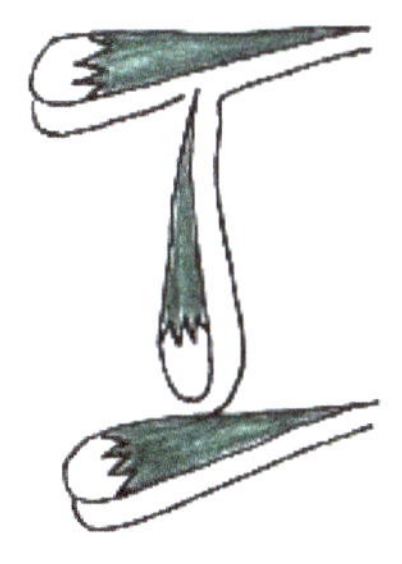

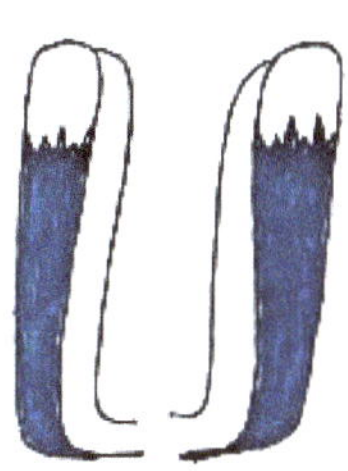

The only reason I made it this far in my life is because

Where are all my African American Queens?

We all view life differently and fall in love with different people, so I guess you could say,

In order to get where I wanted to be in life, I had to move like

We all need your blessings.
GOD
BLESS US
ALL